Other books in this series:
A Feast of After Dinner Jokes   A Romp of Naughty Jokes
A Portfolio of Business Jokes   A Bouquet of Wedding Jokes
A Round of Golf Jokes   A Spread of Over 40s Jokes

Published in the USA in 1992 by Exley Giftbooks
Published in Great Britain in 1992 by Exley Publications Ltd
Cartoons © Bill Stott 1992
Copyright © Helen Exley 1992
ISBN 1-85015-321-3
A copy of the CIP data is available from the British Library on request.
Series Editor: Helen Exley
Editor: Elizabeth Cotton
Cover designed by Pinpoint Design Company
Typeset by Delta, Watford
Printed and bound by Grafo SA – Bilbao, Spain
Exley Publications Ltd, 16 Chalk Hill, Watford, Herts WD1 4BN, United Kingdom.
Exley Giftbooks, 359 East Main Street, Suite 3D, Mount Kisco, NY 10549, USA.

Acknowledgements: The publishers gratefully acknowledge permission to reprint
copyright material. They would be pleased to hear from any copyright holders not
here acknowledged.
Extracts from *Turning 40* by Dave Barry, reprinted by permission of Random House
UK Ltd, Crown Publishing Group, NY and Campbell, Thompson, McLaughlin;
extracts from *The I Hate To Diet Dictionary* by Sandra Bergeson, reprinted by
permission of Turnbull & Willoughby; extracts from *The Dieter's Dictionary,* reprinted
by permission of Slimming Magazine and Argus Books; extracts from *Life's a Bitch . . .
and Then You Diet* by Serena Gray, reprinted by permission of Little, Brown; extracts
from *Just Say A Few Words* by Bob Monkhouse, reprinted by permission of Random
House UK Ltd; extracts from *Miss Piggy's Guide To Life,* reprinted by permission of
Michael Joseph; extract from *Punch* by David Langdon, reprinted by permission of
Punch; extracts from *10,000 Jokes, Toasts and Stories,* reprinted by permission of
Doubleday Inc, NY; extracts from *The Public Speaker's Bible* by Stuart Turner,
reprinted by permission of HarperCollins; extracts from *Jokes, Quotes and One-Liners*
by Herbert V. Prochnow and Herbert V. Prochnow Jr, reprinted by permission of
HarperCollins.

—A BINGE OF—
DIET
•JOKES•

Cartoons by Bill Stott

EXLEY
MT. KISCO, NEW YORK • WATFORD, UK

Fading Willpower!

"I find dieting a losing battle . . . in fact I surrendered years ago!"

P. MACDONALD

*

Willpower is the ability to resist temptation until you can be sure that no-one's looking . . .

*

"**Desperation:** eating the dog's choc drops."

from *The Dieter's Dictionary*

*

"**Abstinence**, n.
Makes the heart grow fonder."

SANDRA BERGESON, from *The I Hate to Diet Dictionary*

*

"Serious dieters do not pinch the baby's rusks."

PAM BROWN

*

"WHO SAYS I'VE GOT NO WILL POWER – I'LL GET THAT PECAN

PIE IF IT'S THE LAST THING I DO"

Food, Glorious Food

Now some women fantasise nightly
Of erotic adventures and steam
But without sounding drab, all I want to grab
Is a bucket or two of ice-cream.

PAM AYRES

*

Waitress: "And what would madam like for dessert?"

Customer: "Three scoops of double chocolate chip real cream ice cream, one scoop of banana and two of vanilla - covered in chocolate fudge sauce..."

Waitress: "And would madam like a few cherries on the top?"

Customer: "No thank you, I'm on a diet."

*

I am constantly in
The mood
For food.

OGDEN NASH

*

"STOP <u>LOOKING</u> AT ME LIKE THAT!"

*

"Dieticians are the worst enemy of the great cuisine. It is impossible to have low calories in excellent food."

LOUIS VAUDABLE

*

"I am not a glutton - I'm an explorer of food."

ERMA BOMBECK

*

"MALCOLM'S GIVEN UP DRINKING AND SMOKING AND GONE ON
A STRICT DIET - HAVEN'T YOU MALCOLM?"

Dieting Can Seriously Damage Your Health

"I went on a diet, swore off drinking and heavy eating, and in fourteen days I lost two weeks."

JOE E. LEWIS

*

"**Unhealthy:** what thin people call you when you are fat and fat people call you when you are thin."

from The Dieter's Dictionary

*

"Weight-watcher Lynda Smethurst, who lost a staggering 168 pounds was unable to collect her prize for 'Dieter of the year' due to the fact that she only weighed 150 pounds when she started her diet . . ."

WILSON DUBOIS

*

"Stay out of bed, and stay active, and eat rice and fish - and eventually you die."

MARLON BRANDO, about his crash diet

*

OTHER PEOPLE EATING

"Contrary to popular opinion, the most uncomfortable aspect of dieting is not the continual need to watch what you eat. The really difficult part is having to watch what other people are eating."

DENIS NORDEN

*

"A true friend shares your diet – even if she *is* a size eight."

PAM BROWN

*

"I'd have no objection to people who eat like sparrows if they'd only stop that everlasting chirping about it."

BOB MONKHOUSE, from *Just Say A Few Words*

*

VITAL STATISTICS

"**Acceptable weight**: what you weigh now if you were six inches taller."

from *The Dieter's Dictionary*

*

"**Adult**: one who has ceased to grow vertically but not horizontally."

ANON

*

"I had no intention of giving her my vital statistics. 'Let me put it this way,' I said. 'According to my girth, I should be a ninety-foot redwood.'"

ERMA BOMBECK

*

"Ideal weight chart: information invoking desire to be a 6ft 4 man."

from *The Dieter's Dictionary*

*

FOREVER HUNGRY

"'The reason you are so fat,' pronounced the psychiatrist, 'is that your whole life is orientated towards eating and drinking. You like parties for the hors-d'oeuvres. A football match to you means hot dogs and beer. Watching television is a long succession of snacks. And...'

'Wait a minute,' interrupted the patient. "Don't you serve anything during psychoanalysis?'"

MOAT WALKER

*

"He said he hoped we had left enough room for tonight's evening meal. I told him I had enough room for the evening meals of the next fortnight."

PETER POOK

*

"I eat when I'm depressed and I eat when I'm happy. When I can't decide whether I'm tired or hungry I make the decision while I'm eating."

OPRAH WINFREY

*

*"WE WERE WONDERING IF WE SHOULDN'T EASE UP ON
GORDON'S DIET, DOCTOR...."*

"THE DOCTOR SAID APPLES WERE NON-FATTENING SO I ATE 68

OF THE LITTLE DEVILS!"

WEDNESDAY

4.14 pm	Two cookies
4.34	One more cookie
4.51	Small handful of peanuts
5.17	Slightly larger handful of peanuts
5.44	The rest of the peanuts
6.11	Crackers with cheese dip
6.32	Breadstick with cheese dip
6.45	Cheese chips with cheese dip
7.10	Small slice of cake from piece left in icebox
7.26	Remainder of cake (really, it is silly to have such a small piece on a big plate taking up so much room)
7.38	One peanut-butter and jelly sandwich
7.42	With potato chips
7.46	And two pickles
8.01	Another cookie
8.11	Remainder of dip on assorted chips, sticks, etc.(it will just have to be thrown out otherwise)
8.37	Two seltzer tablets in glass of water

from *Miss Piggy's Guide to Life*

*

THE TIME TO DIET

"At a Weight Watchers meeting, one woman to another: 'What finally decided me was overhearing my son threatening our neighbour's son with "My mummy's bigger than your mummy."'"

DAVID LANGDON, in *Punch*

*

"NEVER MIND AUNT WINNIE - THAT CHAIR'S BEEN ON ITS WAY OUT FOR YEARS."

"OK - YOU'RE NOT FAT, YOU'RE COMFORTABLE ... MAYBE A LITTLE TOO COMFORTABLE, EH?"

*

"When your daughter hands her maternity dresses on to you, and you are 55, then it's time to think about a diet."

PETER GRAY

*

"Worry when a hippopotamus snorts in greeting."

PAM BROWN

EXCUSES, EXCUSES

- I have heavy bones . . .

- It's coming up to winter and I have to build up reserves of blubber . . .

- Fattening food is cheaper (besides, it tastes better) . . .

- It's just puppy fat . . .

- When I diet my best bumps vanish first – the worst bumps are immovable . . .

- It's because I <u>just</u> had a baby (six years ago . . .)

- It's my metabolism – I just have to <u>look</u> at a cream cake and I put on five pounds . . .

- This pair of jeans has <u>always</u> been too tight . . .

- I'm not overweight – I'm just undertall . . .

*

"YOU CAME DOWN BECAUSE YOU THOUGHT YOU
HEARD BURGLARS? GOT THEM TRAPPED IN THE
REFRIGERATOR HAVE YOU?"

The Secret of Weight Gain . . .

"Have you noticed that some women just don't seem to gain weight, no matter what they eat? You'll be in a restaurant, eating a Diet Plate

consisting of four tunafish molecules garnished
with low-sodium parsley, and you can nevertheless
actually *feel* yourself gaining weight. Meanwhile
at the next table is a woman wearing a size zero
dress, wolfing down a chocolate cake that had to be
delivered to her table via forklift. How does she
get away with it? Where does she put the calories?
The answer is: *into your body*. Yes! If you look
into her purse, you'll find that she, like many
modern weight-conscious women, is carrying an
electronic device called a Calorie Transmaterializer,
which transforms the food entering her body
into invisible rays and shoots them into the body
of whoever is sitting nearby. If you are so
unfortunate as to be sitting near *several* hungry
women with Calorie Transmaterializers, you
could easily explode before they get past
their appetizers. If I were you, I'd get one of these
handy devices *soon*."

DAVE BARRY, from *Turning 40*

*

"I've been on the Valium diet for eight and a half years now. If you take enough Valium it'll help you lose weight. It doesn't really curb your appetite, but most of your food falls on the floor."

GEORGE MILLER

*

"The doctor put me on a staple diet to help me lose weight – but I find paper clips easier to swallow."

MATTHEW BROWN

*

"My wife is on a diet. Coconuts and bananas. She hasn't lost any weight, but can she climb a tree!"

HENRY YOUNGMAN

*

"There's a new Chinese diet. Order all the food you want but use only one chopstick."

BOB MONKHOUSE, from *Just Say a Few Words*

*

She's on a sea-food diet. She only has to see food and she eats it.

*

"HE'S ON A WEEKLY COURSE OF SPECIAL DIET CRACKERS.
THEY'RE USUALLY ALL GONE BY TUESDAY BREAKFAST."

"GOSH! I COULD EAT A HORSE - A HIGH PROTEIN, LOW

CHOLESTEROL, SUGAR FREE HORSE, OF COURSE."

"**Dieter's Law:** food that tastes the best has the highest number of calories."

ROZANNE WEISSMAN

*

"I worry about scientists discovering that lettuce has been fattening all along..."

ERMA BOMBECK

*

"He's on a high-fibre diet - chipboard from DIY shops."

STUART TURNER, from *The Public Speaker's Bible*

*

"So Turner made a fortune?"
"Yes, he invented a chocolate bonbon with a lettuce center for women on a diet."

from *10,000 Jokes, Toasts and Stories*

*

DIETING BLUES

"Eat, drink and be merry, for tomorrow ye diet."
WILLIAM GILMORE BEYMER

*

LIAR!

"**Eve:** only woman ever really tempted by an apple."
from *The Dieter's Dictionary*

*

"The only way to keep your health is to eat what
you don't want, drink what you don't like and do
what you'd rather not."

MARK TWAIN

*

"All the things I like doing are either immoral,
illegal, or fattening."

ALEXANDER WOOLLCUT

DIET? NO THANKS

"The only time he worries about obesity...is when he tries to spell it."

STUART TURNER, from The Public Speaker's Bible

*

"My friend doesn't diet, yet he never puts on an ounce. He eats six meals a day. An average meal consists of three steaks, four pounds of potatoes, three hamburgers, and apple pie, and ice-cream and a sundae. And he still weighs the same thirty-four stone."

from Caper's Weekly

*

"I feel about airplanes the way I feel about diets. It seems to me they are wonderful things for other people to go on."

JEAN KERR

*

"MA! QUICK! DAD'S HAD A RELAPSE!"

"WARNING! YOU HAVE BEEN DETECTED MAKING
UNAUTHORIZED ENTRY TO THE REFRIGERATOR - PLEASE
REPLACE PURLOINED ITEMS IMMEDIATELY!"

Temptation

"The only way to get rid of temptation is to yield to it...I can resist everything but temptation."

OSCAR WILDE

*

"About the only time losing is more fun than winning . . . is when you're fighting temptation."

from It's not will-power I need . . . It's won't power

*

"If it wasn't for wrestling with my conscience . . . I'd get no exercise at all!"

from It's not will-power I need . . . It's won't power

*

"No man in the world has more courage than the man who can stop after eating one peanut."

STUART TURNER, from The Public Speaker's Bible

*

<u>EAT! EAT! EAT!</u>

The average American eats about one and a half tons of food every year.

*

I'm a very light eater . . . when it starts getting light . . . I start eating.

*

"Diet tip: Never eat anything at one sitting that you can't lift."

from *Miss Piggy's Guide to Life*

*

"I eat merely to put food out of my mind."

N. F. SIMPSON

*

"I told my doctor I get very tired when I go on a diet, so he gave me pep pills. Know what happened? I ate faster."

JOE E. LEWIS

DIETS ARE NO GOOD WITHOUT EXERCISE SO HIS DINNER'S ON THE GARAGE ROOF AND I'VE HIDDEN THE LADDER

"EAT THAT LAST PEA AND YOU'RE OVER YOUR CALORIE COUNT."

"Strength is the capacity to break a chocolate bar into four pieces with your bare hands - and then eat just one of the pieces."

JUDITH VIORST

*

"**Abstainer** *n*. A weak person who yields to the temptation of denying himself a pleasure."

AMBROSE BIERCE

*

"The disheartening thing about the average diet is it does so much for the willpower and so little for the waistline."

HERBERT V. PROCHNOW and HERBERT V. PROCHNOW Jr.

*

Take, O take the cream away,
Take away the sugar too;
Let the morning coffee stay
As a black and bitter brew.
I have gained since yesternight -
Shoot the calories on sight!

STODDARD KING

*

"**Diet**, n.

The all-consuming obsession with the
food you shouldn't have eaten yesterday but did,
the food you have eaten today but shouldn't have,
and the food you shouldn't eat tomorrow but
probably will."

SANDRA BERGESON, from *The I Hate to Diet Dictionary*

*

"I've been on a constant diet for the last
two decades. I've lost a total of 789 pounds.
By all accounts, I should be hanging from
a charm bracelet."

ERMA BOMBECK

*

"Let's face it. If your average woman knew as
much about sexual politics as she does about the
number of calories in a slice of cheesecake, this
society would be a matriarchy."

SERENA GRAY, from *Life's A Bitch...and Then You Diet*

*

"MMM! POACHED CARROT!"

"Dieting is like any other addiction. Once you've had that first drink or that first hit, everything about the next drink or the next hit is all settled but the date and time. Once you've been on your first diet, the urge to go on one can come at any moment, in any place, and for any reason.

SERENA GRAY, from *Life's A Bitch...and Then You Diet*

*

READY, STEADY, DIET!

"When you begin to think all plate glass windows distort, it's time to think about a diet."

PAM BROWN

*

"When you have that sinking feeling on a scale, it's time to start reducing."

HERBERT V. PROCHNOW and HERBERT V. PROCHNOW Jr.

*

"THE ABILITY TO LOSE WEIGHT IS ALL IN THE MIND.

UNFORTUNATELY YOU HAVE A FLABBY MIND."

"SEE! I TOLD YOU THAT YOU WERE STILL TOO HEAVY FOR THE

SKIPPING ROUTINE!"

*

"**Panic**, n.

A tight caftan."

SANDRA BERGESON, from *The Hate to Diet Dictionary*

*

"You know you need to diet when they start to charge extra on the airlines..."

PAM BROWN

*

WELCOME TO
LIGHTBODY
HEALTH FARM

THE FAT INVASION

"Why am I bothering to eat this chocolate? I might as well apply it directly to my thighs."

RHODA MORGENSTERN on the *"Mary Tyler Moore Show"*

*

"Our wonderful Human Machine... is made up of countless billions of little things called "cells", and it is the special duty of some of these little body cells to store up fat. And I will say this for them: they do their duty."

ROBERT BENCHLEY

*

"Outside every fat man there is an even fatter man trying to close in."

KINGSLEY AMIS

*

"A woman is a diet just waiting to happen."

SERENA GRAY, from *Life's A Bitch...and Then You Diet*

*

"My advice if you insist on slimming: Eat as much as you like - just don't swallow it."

HARRY SECOMBE

*

"Little and often doesn't mean a trip to the refrigerator every half hour."

PAM BROWN

*

"The best reducing exercise is to shake the head violently from side to side when offered a second helping."

KAY FINCH

*

"You can't lose weight by talking about it. You have to keep your mouth shut."

from *Farmer's Almanac*

*

"Eating is a self-punishment; punish the food instead. Strangle a loaf of Italian bread. Throw darts at a cheesecake. Chain a lamb chop to the bed. Beat up a cookie."

GILDA RADNER

*

"IT'S HERE IN THE HEALTH FARM RULES: 'EATING THE FURNITURE IS THOUGHT OF AS CHEATING'."

"WHY'S DADDY EATING A T.V. DINNER IN THE BACK OF THE CAR,
IN THE GARAGE?"

FAILING AGAIN

"There was only one occasion in my life when I put myself on a strict diet... and it was the most miserable afternoon I've ever spent."

DENIS NORDEN

*

Overheard in Harrods: "Richard was very depressed. He thought he'd lost weight but when he got on the scales this morning he found it was only wishful shrinking."

"Observer" in *Financial Times*

*

"Every so often I lose weight, and, to my utter horror and indignation, I find in the quiet of the night somebody has put it back on."

LORD GOODMAN

*

"I was doing quite well till I got hooked on diet crackers..."

PAM BROWN

*

"To diet: verb always used in the future tense."

from *The Dieter's Dictionary*

*

"Starting on Monday my will will be stronger than brownies,

And anything more than an unsalted egg will seem crude.

My inner-thigh fat and my upper-arm flab will diminish.

My cheeks will be hallowed, my ribs will begin to protrude.

The bones of my pelvis will make their initial appearance –

A testament to my relentless abstention from food, Starting on Monday."

JUDITH VIORST, from *People and other Aggravations*

*

I'll start with fat, or maybe sugar.
I'll start with exercise – perhaps yoga.
I'll start, I'll start . . .
I'll start tomorrow.

S. P. CARP

*

"HELLO? FAT-BUSTERS? MRS. E. FENWICK, 32 HORTON
BOULEVARD, MEMBER NO. 4734 HAS JUST MADE AND IS ABOUT
TO CONSUME A TRIPLE-DECKER HAM SANDWICH."

FASHIONABLE FADS

"In most diets you have to struggle between getting enough roughage in your food and enough food in your roughage."

HERBERT V. PROCHNOW and HERBERT V. PROCHNOW Jr.

*

"1st woman – So what does this really expensive, no sugar, no calories, no protein, no fat, no carbohydrate diet drink actually contain?

2nd woman – Well . . . water."

WILSON DUBOIS

*

"If you have formed the habit of checking on every new diet that comes along, you will find that, mercifully, they all blur together, leaving you with only one definite piece of information: french fried potatoes are out."

JEAN KERR

*

"MMM - I BET IT ALSO MAKES GREAT WALLPAPER PASTE!"

"Liquid diets - the powder is mixed with water and tastes exactly like powder mixed with water."

ART BUCHWALD

*

"Quite often the part of the body to lose weight first in a fashionable diet is the brain."

PETER GRAY

*

"It's no good tiptoeing up to the bathroom scales -
they hear you coming."

PAM BROWN

*

"There's one thing that will give you more
for your money than it would ten years ago -
the penny scale."

HERBERT V. PROCHNOW and HERBERT V. PROCHNOW Jr.

*

*"I'LL JUST GIVE THE SCALES A QUICK FLICK - DUST CAN WEIGH
TONS, YOU KNOW...."*

"WILL YOU LOOK AT THAT! I'VE LOST .37542 OF A POUND!"

"Do not weigh yourself constantly. Every time you stand on the scales it stretches the little springs and wing nuts inside and slowly presses them flat - the result, *even with no weight gain whatsoever,* is that the scale makes you appear to weigh a little more each time."

from *Miss Piggy's Guide to Life*

*

"WILL YOU STILL LOVE ME WHEN I'M SYLPH-LIKE?"

Wasting Away

"So I think it is very nice for ladies to be lithe and lissome,
But not so nice that you cut yourself if you happen to embrace or kissome."

OGDEN NASH

*

"In order to help me maintain my diet, I decided to chart my weight loss on a graph. With the added incentive, the pounds melted away; but as the graph plummeted downwards, my temper became increasingly frayed.

My understanding husband bore the brunt of my ill-humour without complaint - until one memorable morning when I goaded him too far. He picked up the graph, studied it for a moment, then remarked quietly: 'If this trend continues, you should disappear in exactly four months' time.'"

M. MORRISON

*

"THERE'S SOMETHING IN IT FOR YOU IF YOU CAN GET A COUPLE
OF STEAKS UNDER MY DOOR."

DON'T FEED THE GUESTS

"Letter to a friend from a man at a health farm: 'Help! Send me a file with a cake in it.'"

SUNNY O'NEIL

*

"A customer, . . . surrounded by stripped pine and natural food, was offended by a little vase of plastic flowers on his table. 'We have to use plastic flowers,' the owner told him. "If we use real flowers, the customers eat them.'"

GARY DUNFORD

*

"One popular health farm has found that it's a good idea to keep slimming guests occupied with arts and crafts between exercise courses and special meals. The art class is proving extremely popular. One week the first prize went to an oil painting of a fully stocked refrigerator."

R. S.

*

"**Bathroom scales:** equipment which only seems to work correctly when one holds on to towel rail, stands on one foot and leans hard to the left."

from *The Dieter's Dictionary*

*

"**Scale, How to use A,**

When using the home scale, these simple rules must be followed:

1. Always place the scale on thick shag carpeting (it would be more beneficial to place it under 4½ feet of water, but this is often difficult in a bathroom and is very hard on scales).

2. Hold tightly onto the sink or shower rod (both when possible) and gradually release the weight of the body onto the scale.

3. Make sure needle placement is accurate by cautiously adjusting the little round knob on the center-front, very slowly to the left. (Zero is a wide number and should be treated accordingly.)

WARNING: Stay away from digital scales. (They are not properly adjustable and therefore inaccurate.)"

SANDRA BERGESON, from *The I Hate to Diet Dictionary*